Go

God in Ward 12

RICHARD BEWES

LUTTERWORTH PRESS
GUILDFORD AND LONDON

First published in Great Britain 1973

ISBN 0 7188 2027 4

Printed in Great Britain by
Hunt Barnard Printing Ltd., Aylesbury, Bucks.

To the staff and patients of Harold Wood Hospital

Biblical quotations are from the Revised Standard Version

CONTENTS

I

WHO GAVE US HOSPITALS?

Silently I stood looking at the girl who lay motionless in the little room. She had been in her early twenties, a vivacious personality they told me. Now she was dead. A car had skidded . . . There were five of us in the mortuary – the two grief-stricken parents, a couple of policemen, and myself.

My mind went back to the shrill summons of the telephone that had shattered my slumber in the early hours a week earlier. A call at three a.m. was it? Groping for the receiver I had croaked out "Yes?" At that hour it's about all the response you can manage.

"Mr Bewes? It's the hospital. There's been an accident. The relatives are here . . . " Dazedly one starts to clamber into clothes discarded four hours earlier. "What's the matter?" comes a sleepy mumble from the other side of the bed.

"It's the hospital," I explain softly. "I won't be long, Liz." I tiptoe on to the landing, taking care not to wake the children; down the stairs and out into the cold of a

February night. The rattle of the garage doors sounds like thunder in the chill silence. The Morris Traveller explodes into life with a harsh cacophany of sound that banishes the last vestige of sleep from me; and I'm snaking my way along the half-mile stretch that separates us from the local hospital, the headlights heightening the unusual desolation of the empty road. The fight for the girl's life is already on at the hospital casualty section. I back the car into a convenient recess, and in a few seconds am once again trudging that familiar corridor. I check that my hip pocket Bible is with me as I prepare to meet the girl's parents and pray with them. It's come in handy before . . .

And now a week later the fight was over. I had been in several times and the patient had never recovered consciousness. "Would you like me to pray with you?" I suggested now. The girl's father nodded and held his wife a little closer as together they bowed their heads. The policemen, I noticed, kept their eyes open – ready perhaps to lend a steadying hand, I guessed. "O God" – I began. This kind of praying is never easy. How futile it seemed just now. Bring in the parson when there's nothing more to be done and there's just a battered body to be prayed over. As I looked at the girl's face, peaceful now in death, I reflected: I wonder whether anyone ever really fought for your soul when you were alive, as the doctors have fought for your body these last seven days? A stranger to the family, I could never know the answer to that one. The prayer over, we spoke for a while, made a tentative agreement to meet again, shook hands and went our different ways – they to arrange the funeral, me to hold a staff-meeting with my colleagues in the North-East London parish where we work.

What, it may be asked, is the relevance of Christ and the Gospel in all this? In the ups and downs of a part-time hospital chaplaincy? With its comings and goings, its uncertainties and sadnesses, its fantastic turn-over of patients and all the trappings and departments of the National Health Service and the Welfare State?

"It isn't that I've got any quarrel with what you folk are doing," a young salesman once said to me from his hospital bed. "But I just don't see where it's getting you."

Or there was the middle-aged woman with her parting chirp: "Bye, Vicar. Nice talking to you." And then her aside to the next bed: "Poor thing!"

A right sense of history alone immediately explodes the myth that hospitals can do without Christ and His message. Across the world, hospitals owe their very existence directly to Jesus Christ. In England and America today atheists and agnostics receiving treatment in hospital are themselves benefitting from a culture built over the centuries on Christian standards and ideals that demand care and love for the sick, the elderly and the afflicted. Our hospitals today may be nationalized, but it wasn't a state department that began them! Indeed, with the current decline in faith and Christ-centred service, hundreds of our hospitals find themselves – though superbly equipped – hopelessly understaffed. It seems already apparent that our medical service cannot get along without Christians.

Before the time of Christ there were no real hospitals as such. Most medical work was undertaken by professional private physicians on behalf of the rich. It was the Christian era that brought about the emergence of the hospital as a place of refuge and care for the common victim of disease and accident. By the fourth century it was known that due to Christians within the Roman Empire, hospitals had been established for lepers, cripples and those generally afflicted. The world's first nursing order was probably that of the St Augustine nuns. In pioneer missionary work in many lands Christian men and women have been found willing to give of their abilities and medical skill in a thousand different unknown backwaters, with the Word of God as their strength, and the love of Christ as their motivation.

Christ and the Hospital. The two will always be found together. Some of the ways in which the power of the living Lord is brought to bear upon the world of medicine and healing is the subject of the chapters that follow.

2

ALL ON ONE LEVEL

Cups of tea at the crack of dawn, supper at tea time, libraries on wheels, Lucozade and grapes, blanket baths and screens – life in hospital has a routine and a cliché-ridden lingo all of its own. "What I say is, you can always look round and see someone worse than yourself" – "Well, I suppose it's just one of those things" – "Never had a day's illness in my life till I came here" – "I don't know what I've done to deserve this" – "There's no place like home, you know" – "Ah well, these things are sent to try us".

No doubt about it, hospital is a great leveller, reducing rich and poor, tea-boy and tycoon alike to a single pyjama-clad category. Banteringly I once accused my two brothers of only seeing people "professionally" in this way. One of them, a surgeon, would, I always insisted, view people in the mass simply as "Patients". The other brother worked at one time in British Railways. "Now you," I insisted, "can't help lumping together any crowd you see as just 'Passengers'." Then they both turned on me. "But you're worse than either of us," one of them retorted, "you patronizingly see all of us lot as your 'Congregation'!" Humbly I had to agree!

"*Now I suppose you're going to convert me,*" said the middle-aged woman facing an operation. Evidently she too suspected me of treating her as part of my hospital "flock". I paused. "I could never convert anyone in fact," I finally replied, "only God can really touch and change a person's heart." What that lady, however, would not have guessed is the amazing frequency with which God chooses to do just that in the levelling environment of a General Hospital.

Take Bernard Hartley for example – an outstanding predecessor of mine in the ministry of the parish where I am Vicar. Living in retirement nearby, he was taken ill and spent some weeks in our hospital. In the bed next to him was a member of the local Humanist Association. As patients together the two men conversed on many subjects during those weeks, the one an elderly clergyman now in his eighties, the other an atheist of about forty. After Bernard Hartley's discharge, his companion spoke to me of their talks together. "It's been an experience talking to that man," he confessed. "Deep down he's got something that I've never had. I've been made to think in these last weeks as I've not been made to think in years. Why, he even got me looking up verses of the Bible that he wrote down for me to do homework on. Talking to him has been like . . . " – he reflected a moment – " . . . it's been like coming back to the Rock."

Patients they may all be, but God's people are there among them, and I do not mean simply clergy or full-time Christian workers. Take the case of Olive, one of our own church members.

There had been concern about Olive's health for some time. A housewife in her late thirties she had found God only a couple of years previously – "It all began with a talk I heard on the radio by the Archbishop of Canterbury," she once confessed. A book by Billy Graham and the help of a neighbour had helped to clinch her decision. She had quickly become known and accepted by the other church members as one of Christ's people. Now, it appeared, she had a form of cancer. It was going to mean an operation. The prayers of many began to converge upon her. Later, when the operation was successfully over she told me, "Those prayers, they were marvellous, really marvellous; I felt absolutely lifted up by them and I had no fear or trepidation. I felt I was in God's hands." But that wasn't all.

In Olive's ward a girl had been brought in, called Eileen. She had been involved in a severe road accident. In great pain, she was to spend several weeks in traction. Olive began to pray for Eileen in her distress, and a bond grew between the two patients, which developed into a friendship that was to outlast the hospital stay. Later on came the day when Olive was able to lead Eileen to a personal commitment of her life to Christ – simply through conversation and prayer together. Eileen was confirmed in our church a year later.

Perhaps I get the best of both worlds, the parish and the hospital together. In larger hospitals there are full-time resident chaplains. Theirs is the harder task, for the bulk of those they contact they will never meet again, and they may rarely know the extent to which any one patient was reached by God's love during a hospital stay. But I can look round our church fellowship and repeatedly see faces – singing happy faces – of those whose initial contact with the church was made in hospital, as likely as not through a fellow-patient who "happened to be there" – and cared. Let none of Christ's disciples ever imagine that when they have to go into hospital they are simply to be on the receiving end. There will be work for them to do.

"Oh, I'm just aching to leave this world," an elderly saint once confided to me in her ward. Beside her on the locker I saw her large well-thumbed Bible. If ever a Bible had been loved to death it was that one; it was practically loose-leaf by now! She had her own "Language of Zion" terminology for everything. "Journeying mercies" for her would have meant, in modern parlance, a window seat in the middle of the train and back to the engine! She had given her life to God's service, and here she was, over seventy, longing to die. Rightly or wrongly I pulled her up. "Don't lie down and die," I urged, "don't give up before God's ready for you. Remember, there's plenty for you to do by your prayers alone in this place. The one person who would like you to die before your time is the Devil. After all he's called the Murderer in Scripture. What he'd like is to get you out of the way as soon as possible and stop those prayers of yours! So don't satisfy his wishes by giving up and longing to die." The elderly saint looked very astonished for a moment. Then she said simply, "I'll stop thinking like that." It was the last time I was to see her.

Now I suppose you're going to convert me. Funnily

enough it just doesn't work out like that. In the last analysis Christianity is caught as much as taught, and what better place than a hospital ward in which to pick up the infection of the Gospel?

3

A GAME OF CARDS

The telephone rang for the umpteenth time. Mechanically I picked up the receiver and recognized the voice of a neighbouring Vicar. "Richard? Peter here. Look, someone's been converted through one of your ward services . . . " Converted? I thought wryly of the tired piano that accompanies our brave church team of hospital singers. With voices that at ten o'clock on a Sunday morning haven't fully woken up yet! The faithful little cardboard box of hymn books. And . . . and . . .

But the voice on the phone was still speaking. " . . . He's from our parish you see. No I don't know him, he doesn't go to church at all . . . Well, that's it – I've been visiting one or two of our members in hospital and ran up against him. He certainly seems to have found a faith in Christ. And look – he wants to meet the man who gave the talk in that ward service. It was just recently, on Sunday. His name's Charles . . . " I did some checking. Yes, it was a Sunday in February 1970.

And – let's do some working out – the speaker on that occasion was, well now it was Robbie.

Robbie is my next door neighbour. Hailing from Islington in earlier days he had moved to our parish when it was little more than a village on the outskirts of London. His chief social interests had revolved around the pub and greyhound racing. And then in 1950 a mission had been held in the area, and Robbie heard the call of Christ in a guest night service for the first time.

> "Behold, I stand at the door and knock; if anyone hears my voice and opens the door, I will come in to him and eat with him, and he with me" (Revelation 3: 20).

The visiting preacher had been a young man, John Stott by name, now well known as the Rector of All Soul's, Langham Place. That evening set Robbie, and Frances his wife, firmly on the path of discipleship, service and leadership in God's Church. What a strength there is in the testimony of Christian laymen! A number of our church members take their turn at speaking in public, and we could do with more of them in the church at large. Men unafraid to get up and speak in practical everyday terms of a God Who is alive today . . .

But forward again twenty years to the ward service on that cold Sunday morning in February. In fact the venerable piano wasn't used that day! Two or three contemporary hymns with guitar, a reading, some prayers. Then Robbie was on his feet, over fifty years of age now, but with the quick thinking and repartee that seems to characterize folk from Islington. The east London accent was still there in the text as it was read out:

> "Before I was afflicted I went astray; but now I keep thy word . . . It is good for me that I was afflicted, that I might learn Thy statutes" (Psalm 119: 67, 71).

In the few minutes available the theme was developed, one of comfort and hope for those prepared to let God speak to them in and through the experience of sickness and pain. C. S. Lewis has expressed it well in *The Problem of Pain* – "God whispers to us in our pleasures, speaks in our consciences, but shouts in our pains: it is His megaphone to rouse a deaf world." The message this Sunday was the same, if couched in different terms and with ample use of illustration and story. "If," concluded Robbie, "your stay in this hospital proves to be the means by which you found your way back to God, then one day you too will say, 'It was good for me that I was afflicted, that I might learn Thy statutes . . .' ".

Many of the patients had listened with interest, but four men – "up-patients" – seated at a table behind the speaker, had affected vast indifference to the proceedings and continued throughout with a game of cards, only pausing occasionally to offer a sarcastic witticism. One of them was Charles.

Charles was a short, dark-haired man from a nearby housing estate. He was in hospital for a serious operation and he was worried about it, knowing that his chances of survival were about fifty-fifty. His attitude may have been one of careless contempt, but his features were pinched and drawn as he dealt the cards that Sunday morning, and Robbie's voice behind him was not merely the background sound to his game that an onlooker might have imagined.

Several days later – "D'you remember me?" Robbie was saying to him. Charles shook his head. "I can't say I do." Of course! He had sat right behind the speaker in that ward service, had never even glanced in his direction! Robbie prompted his memory. "I'm the bloke who gave the talk in that service here the other day. Someone told me you wanted to see me." The short man's face lit up. A hand was thrust out. "I'm glad to have met you! I've been trying to find out who you were!" He began to tell of his experience. "Those words from the Bible that you spoke about – the more I thought about them the surer I was that they were true. I wasn't really thinking about the card game," he confessed, "I believe I lost every hand I played." Charles readily testified of his deliberate commmitment to Christ before going down to the operating theatre.

Apparently the operation had been entirely successful, and the patient, happy in his new-found faith, was making a good recovery. Several resolves were made. About telling his work mates of the step that he had taken. And the family – though would they understand? Charles had some doubts about that. There would be church too – "I'm looking forward to that." A couple of days later the two men met again, and Charles was steadily improving and was unshakable in his conviction that he had begun with God. No doubt there would be problems ahead, he admitted, but he had a real sense of peace with his Maker. "And," he beamed, "they're letting me go home on Saturday."

But it was not to be. On Friday there was a sudden relapse and Charles the card-player was dead. The deterioration was quite unexpected and before anyone could intervene he was gone, into eternity with no warning. A tragedy? There was his family of course. Not to mention the church family who had already been looking forward to welcoming a new Christian in their midst. Our prayer fellowship had been getting ready for him . . . "Perhaps it was just God's time for him," said Robbie when it happened. "In which case we can only thank Him for His mercy in leading Charles to Himself before calling him away."

Hundreds of people every year come under the sound of God's message of love and forgiveness in our ward services. Charles was only one of them, a little man facing an operation and whiling away a Sunday morning with a game of cards. It could have been you . . .

4

TRANSISTORIZED MINISTRY

When I was at theological college I acquired my first tape recorder. It was one of those Grundigs, an ancient secondhand machine, but it gave useful service for some years. Not that I was particularly ambitious with it, but at least I rose above the "Record-the-children's-voices-surprise-your-friends-at-the-party" level. And then a few months after our marriage we were burgled one night. Several things went. A camera, a convector heater, a record player, a radio – the usual sort of things; and also the ancient Grundig.

Amazingly we had taken out full insurance on these items only four days beforehand. "That's all right," the broker had said, "send us the premium when you're ready. But you can reckon you're covered as from now." He was a good fellow; he stumped up all right, even though our premium arrived in his office only ten minutes before our claims for over two-hundred pounds!

I suppose I'd have gone on with the Grundig, a fine

domestic recorder, had we not had that burglary. As it was, I took some advice from a tape recording professional, and bought a Uher. That Uher was a dream. A little transistorized thing, weighing only six pounds or so, with four speeds and a superb quality of reproduction, it had won an international award and was regularly used by BBC reporters for outside broadcasts. It gave me virtually a new dimension in tape recording. I began to experiment, to create, to worry about such factors as "wow and flutter", "print-through" and "drop-out". I took a tape recording magazine every month. All with one purpose in view – to use this thing for the Kingdom of God.

I hadn't been appointed Chaplain in our hospital a month before I learnt about a little group of dedicated young people who sat in a studio rigged up in the hospital every Sunday afternoon. Their idea was a simple one, to channel radio programmes, chiefly of pop music, through to the headphone sets beside every patient's bed. The Hospital League of Friends had generously blown £500 on the project, and the studio was pretty well equipped with record turntables, tape decks, microphones, a mixer and over a thousand records. And there was me with a Uher . . .

"Words of Life" was the name of our first programme series, and was kindly received by the Hospital radio group. The whole thing had been pre-recorded at the Vicarage. By that time I'd had to get another tape recorder, a big mains machine this time, a Brenell Mk. V. I'd put together a small record turntable in the Vicarage after a bit of trial and error (my first attempt caught fire!), and there we were ready to go – "The only radio programme in England based in a Vicarage!", came the brash claim over the hospital headphones. And perhaps it was too.

In the early days "Words of Life" took literally hours to put together. It was a half-hour programme of Christian music, personality features, news items and a six minute talk. Our own church members were regularly involved in the programme, and "The Words of Life" singing group began to record musical items for inclusion on the weekly broadcast. Clicks and unnecessary material would have to be edited out of the tape of course. I began to develop a "thing" about passing cars, horrible dogs with persistent barks, ice cream vans, overhead jets and telephone bells.

There is a sort of break-through point in the development of a tape recording enthusiast. It comes when he is willing to chop up his precious tapes and start splicing. To begin with it seems a sacrilegious crime. But it is the secret of creating a programme that moves along with zip, precision and interest. The professionals produce smart little splicing kits, some of which are laboriously time-consuming to use. I use the simple EMI editing block, which is easily the best. That, and a razor blade and roll of Scotch splicing tape (never use sellotape!).

The idea is to cut the tape at an angle of about forty-five degrees, remove the unwanted section of tape, ensure that the two ends of tape are together but not overlapping, and join them with a shortish length of splicing tape. Having done thousands of splices now, I can do the job as easily as picking apples off a tree. Actually even without a block you can do an *ad hoc* splice with a pair of nail scissors. As the join won't be so exact, however, it is wise in such cases to avoid 'sticky' splices by the application of a little talcum powder (my wife's Avon "Elegance" does the trick!).

Of course disaster may strike occasionally! In his enthusiasm the tape editor may chop out more than he intended, and then has to burrow in the waste bin amid a tangle of other rejected loose ends to find that elusive piece that he wants to splice *back* again. Or the razor blade may suddenly turn magnetic, creating further havoc with every snip. After priding myself on making one blade last two months, I was kindly informed by a BBC editor that a new razor blade should be used for every programme!

When the tape was complete I would bring it along to the hospital studio. In those earlier days, before life got more complicated, I would often stay and listen to the tape as the disc jockey for the evening played it through. I recall, on my first visit, seeing the notices of instructions pasted up over the control panel. WATCH YOUR LEVEL. And underneath, NO SPITTING.

The initial "Words of Life" programme was well received. Mind you, we'd put all our best eggs into that first basket. Pancho Gonzales, the great tennis player, once said "Start fast! In the opening point of the match serve your speediest and try and score a clean ace first time." The principle is a good one even if keeping the standard up proves demanding. So we began with the best songs the singing team could muster, a fine interview, "Peter and Sylvia" a singing duo presented by two church members, and a good gravelly voice from Jim, one of our members, who was to take a reading.

Poor Jim was taken ill within a day or two of making the recording, and was hospitalized just in time to hear his own reading!

Technique and presentation improved over the weeks. We would occasionally include "commercials" in the programme, publicizing Bible reading aids and Christian literature of various kinds. News flashes would be read against a background of a clattering typewriter, in order to convey an impression of hectic editorial activity. Sometimes a special guest would be introduced to the programme. Cliff Richard has been down to visit us on more than one occasion, and each time of course has figured prominently on "Words of Life".

The hospital radio DJ's were models of patient kindness towards us. I tend to be a "last minuter", and many times have rushed into the studio to find the DJ sitting at the controls with an air of Olympian calm, ready to slap the tape on to the machine with barely seconds left to zero hour. On one occasion the take-up spool on the studio tape recorder failed, and the operator had to watch twelve hundred feet of tape spill all over the floor, and at the end of the programme wind it patiently back again by hand.

Letters and cards began to come in from enthusiastic listeners to "Words of Life". Evidently the programme was meeting a need.

> " . . . Very many thanks for this evening, we all in this ward listened in and enjoyed it greatly . . . "; "We enjoyed the singing as it was modern" (seven signatures); "May I congratulate you on running such a lively and well-produced programme"; "Sincere

thanks and appreciation for your radio programme – it has been a great comfort to me during my spell in hospital"; "It is a real tonic to hear such programmes, and only wish there were more like them . . . "

Our programmes developed still further, until we were also presenting a weekly Christian DJ programme, "Sacred Spin". A more recent addition has been a fifteen minute mid-week spot entitled "Time to Think". This all naturally involves greater pressure on one's time – particularly in a parish like ours with 13,000 people. One simply begins to think faster, to work faster and to use up the odd quarters of an hour that occur in between other assignments. A whole room in the Vicarage has been turned into what we grandly call "The Production Room". There the equipment is laid out ready for use; egg boxes line the walls and ceiling to offset unwanted echo, and a tape library has been organized. A major advance was made in late 1972 when we began to build a new studio adjoining the church, and found the "boffin" we had been looking for so long, Tony, a church member with a flair for electronics. In one fell swoop we had found a studio manager and had got our spare room back! For six years I'd been fulfilling the rôle of programme producer, script-writer, recording engineer, editor and DJ. The change was none too soon. 1972 was also the year when we acquired the legendary Revox A77 tape recorder. But that's another story.

Hospital radio is only a handmaid to the general spiritual ministry that chaplains can carry out. It cannot stand alone. But in conjunction with ward services and the face-to-face encounter that personal visits make possible, it adds an important dimension to the spiritual life and community ethos of a hospital. "I know your voice," a woman patient suddenly exclaimed as I talked by the next bed with her neighbour, "you're the 'Words of Life' man! You know" – she continued – "I feel as though I really know you people who come on the programme. People like Peter and Sylvia who sing the duets; they've become a part of my life in hospital."

On other occasions someone or other will stop me during a ward visit. "Come here a minute, will you? Look I heard your programme last night. The young girl announcer was saying something about a free booklet on Christianity that you were offering this week. Can I have one?" So someone *was* listening! In fact, provided our publicity is going at full swing, we can get an audience of up to eighty percent listening in. And something is evidently achieved in those commercials, the "young girl announcer" being none other than Liz my wife. "Go on, put some honey into your voice, darling," I urge her anxiously during the recording. Somehow in between our giggling the job gets done. And, amazingly, someone responds! Thank you, God!

A nurse eyed one woman reading a booklet one of us had given her. Its title "How Can I find God?" had excited her interest. "May I borrow that when you've finished with it?" she asked. Later on she handed it back critically. "It seems to me that they're asking too much," was her comment. "But that's the point," came the instant rejoinder from the patient, herself at the threshold of real discipleship, "They're asking *everything*."

Our efforts have not been without effects in other quarters. The potential of hospital radio has been recognized by church workers in many parts of the country, and some sharing of ideas has been possible. God also used the contact with our own hospital radio station to start the ball rolling in a spiritual direction for one or two of its members. Two of its earliest programme chiefs eventually made a start with Christ. I asked one of them, "What was it like coming to church for the first time, when you had never been in your life before?" "Well," he replied, "I did what you do at a big banquet when you watch the people on each side of you to discover what knife and fork to use! That's what I did in church, only hoping that nobody was watching me."

Electronics and the transistor are not, of course, the answer to the problem of communication in the seventies. Techniques and good ideas of themselves achieve precisely nothing in God's purposes. "Some boast of chariots, and some of horses," wrote the Psalmist, "but we boast of the name of the Lord our God." It is all too easy, in a day when the pressures are on, to pin one's faith to machines and equipment – to boast, if you like, of Uher tape recorders and of oxidized polyester sliding past tape heads at seven and a half inches a second. *The Gospel itself must be there* – the real Gospel centering in a Christ Who historically lived, died, and rose again, and whose delight it is to send His Spirit into people's lives and personalities as they put their trust in Him. Unless we have a vital message to share, we might as well pack all our equipment and put up our shutters. There is the first necessity – *content*. It is no good communicating unless we have something to say. The second necessity is *contact*. It is not the slightest use communicating to people who aren't there! Hence the need for attractive well-designed publicity and literature. And for a team of dedicated visitors, intent through friendship and concern to win for the Gospel an audience which, though captive already, lives in a permanent No Man's land between the pillow and the telly! A third necessity is *clarity*. It's no use communicating in yesterday's terms. If we're to tackle the opportunity of hospital radio with any seriousness we must realize that we shall be in competition with the standards set by the most progressive broadcasting corporation in the world. Fourthly there must be *construction*. It's no use communicating without a steady plan and purpose. The "box-of-gimmicks" parson wins only cynical contempt from a society that has seen everything already. Underlying all real Christian communication must be a God-centred strategy that has been soaked in prayer.

The Gospel – and prayer; it really boils down to that ultimately. Perhaps this is where the full-time hospital chaplain needs more support than us part-timers. A parish man can count on a measure of prayer backing in the work he leads, whether in the everyday ministry of his church, or in the more specialized field of a hospital. The full-time chaplain all too often is out on a limb, lacking the ready-made powerhouse that a living church fellowship can afford him. Is there anybody praying for our hospital chaplains today? This is surely the secret of all true ministry, transistorized or not – an unashamed confidence in the dynamic of the Gospel, backed by a vigorous, practical belief that prayer is the most important thing we shall ever accomplish on this earth.

5

ENCOUNTER IN WARD 12

"Richard, I'm terribly sorry, but I'll be out of action for the Vicar's XI this month." John, one of my colleagues, had fluid on the knee, and we discussed the matter at our Monday morning staff meeting. Once a year I have to turn out for a Saturday morning game of football – or to be more precise, half a game, as I usually retire at half time and bring on a substitute. The Vicar's XI against the young people of the church is a sure guarantee of the inclusion of a little spice and needle for our Spring programme, a happy interlude to brighten up the austerity of Lent! All three clergy must turn out for such a gala occasion of course, and I nervously begin my annual rummage of the wardrobe for my hockey boots. The score is duly announced in pontific tones to the congregation on Sunday, even if I conveniently have to forget to name the winning team!

And now John was out of the game. In fact he was to be out of action altogether for the next three weeks, as the doctor had diagnosed a slipped cartilage, and an operation on the knee would be necessary. Re-adjustments to the diary were made at our staff meeting and John prepared himself for a visit to Ward 12 of the hospital, not as a visiting clergyman, but as a patient. A date was fixed, and on Tuesday, March 8th at 11 a.m. John walked into Ward 12.

Barbara was half-way through her nursing training, and not doing too badly at it. She liked the easy informality of the hospital and she got on pretty well with the other trainees. But . . . there was something that troubled her in the women's ward where she was working. It wasn't exactly the work, and it wasn't really to do with the patients as such; she had a tolerably easy bunch just now. It was, she sighed to herself, a problem that had been brought to the forefront of her thinking through the arrival of Jill in the ward.

Jill was in her early twenties. She was brought in with an incurable brain disease, and Barbara was given direct charge of her. There seemed to be something special about this patient, Barbara thoughtfully reflected. It wasn't merely that Jill was a Christian; she gave every indication of living up to it, and Barbara was impressed in spite of herself. Not that she was irreligious exactly; it was simply that the Bible and church didn't grab her. But here was a person near her own age who did go in for Christianity in earnest, a person, Barbara decided, who was good. Then why was she dying? "She mustn't die," thought Barbara to herself, "If God really exists and can see Jill's goodness He won't let her die. Not a good person like her. And only a little over twenty at that."

But Jill did die. Shortly afterwards, on a men's

orthopaedic ward, Barbara found herself nursing an eleven-year-old boy with a broken leg. A rare complication set in and the boy unexpectedly died. And that made Barbara angry. "Who is this God Who takes life when He pleases? Is there anybody there at all? What's the purpose of it all anyway?" Anger turned to depression. The ward sister noticed it. A change would be a good thing perhaps; take her out of herself; different surroundings. Accordingly one morning Barbara was told that she would be transferred to another ward. Early in March she began her new work in Ward 12 . . .

Vijay was writing in his diary. Only a few months back he had turned from Hinduism to Christianity, and regularly he would write down the lessons and experiences encountered in his new-found faith. He had come to England from his home in India a few years back, and had a good job in engineering. He was to help check the plans of the Q.E.2. He was a member of the British Nuclear Energy Society. He had a most attractive wife and things were going well for him.

The change in his beliefs had come about "through mere curiosity". He had seen a crowd of bowler-behatted gentlemen striding with purposeful intention through Bishopsgate near his office in the lunch-hour one Tuesday. "You have heard how curiosity killed the cat!" Vijay later bubbled to his friends. "In my case it opened up to me a new life. I followed those business-men along Bishopsgate – followed them right into a church! And once I was in I couldn't get out!" A crowd of about five hundred had gathered for the weekly Tuesday lunch-hour service at St. Helen's, the most ancient church in the City of London. The atmosphere was informal and coffee was served on the premises. Packets of sandwiches were opened. Every week Dick Lucas the Rector, "a man's man", speaks to the businessmen of London, in their own terms, about the relevance of dynamic New Testament Christianity.

Vijay the Hindu sat there drinking it in. The theme that day was Justification. "I had never heard anything like it before – that God could accept me with all my failings just as I am, because of Jesus' death on the Cross. Up to that time I thought that Jesus had only died for Christians! Now I learnt that He had died for me too. I walked out of that place a Christian."

But now a few months later Vijay was faced with the possibility that he had cancer of the spine. The specialists were making tests. Vijay wrote in his diary on February 7th, "If I were in India, it is most likely that people would say that this was a punishment from God for becoming a Christian. But I think God has been most gracious and loving towards me. If I were not a Christian, or, let me say, if I hadn't left my life with Christ, I would most certainly have panicked. If this had happened last year I wouldn't have had the courage to face it. But today I am bold . . . " A few weeks later Vijay was sent to hospital. He came to ours. The entry in his diary reads, "Friday, March 11th: Admitted to Hospital. Ward 12. At 11 a.m."

On Tuesday, March 15th, I walked into Ward 12. I was bringing Communion round the wards for those who had requested it. We get quite an assortment of communicants on these occasions. Hospital life being what it is, I am sure that some folk put their names down for Communion without quite knowing what they have asked for! On this day the assistant matron who was accompanying me round the wards frowned at the piece of paper in her hand. "Two for Ward 12," she informed me. "There's your assistant from the church. And – it looks like an Indian name." The ward sister drew back the screen. "Here they are, all ready." "Hullo John," I said, "and who's your friend?"

The two of them had met up almost immediately Vijay had arrived. John had been talking to one of his neighbours and the subject of the Church had come up. Presently Vijay padded over. "I'm Vijay," he beamed, "I heard you talking. Do you know I used to be a Hindu; now I'm a Christian! Pleased to meet you." John and Vijay proved good publicity agents for the "Words of Life" broadcast, making sure that the other patients knew when the programme was due. For the next twenty Sundays two records would inevitably be requested on the hospital radio request show; "Life is Wonderful" by The Ambassadors and "You'd better get on that Road," by the Bryan Gilbert Group. They were the only Christian records Vijay knew! The DJs back in the studio bore it all philosophically. Barbara the nurse, however, found her preconceptions being challenged the longer she worked in Ward 12.

So often it happens like that. It is not intellectual arguments conducted on the clever-clever level that swing the battle so much as the testimony of a changed life. It was Sir Henry Holland, the famous missionary eye doctor of India who once said, "If we Christians don't out-live and out-love, we don't deserve to win." Barbara was held by a certain reality and depth about the faith of John and Vijay. She observed too the quality of fellowship enjoyed between them and other members of the church who came in at visiting times. John went home after about three weeks, but Vijay was ordered complete rest flat on his back. One of Barbara's nursing colleagues asked one day, "Vijay, how long have you been here?"

"About seventeen weeks."

"Seventeen weeks? You must be bored stiff!"

"No, I'm not bored; I'm reading the Bible. You know I never had a Bible until a few months ago. In fact I never even *saw* a Bible when I was in India. Do you read the Bible?"

The nurse turned helplessly to her companion. "He must be nuts, he wants to know whether I read the Bible!"

Vijay read the whole Bible during his twenty-week stay in Ward 12. Susheila his wife, still a Hindu, would come in to visit him and laugh softly. "You're enjoying it here, aren't you? Don't want to come back home, do you?" One afternoon Dick Lucas made the trip from town to come and see the patient he had come to know at the lunch-time services at St. Helen's. "Dick! Dick!" The shout rang out to greet him from the far end of the ward. "Why do you think the Old Testament is the Word of God?"

"Well, I don't know, Vijay. You tell me."

"It's because here in the Bible we find a God completely different to all the gods I have ever read about in Hindu and Islamic books. You couldn't *invent* a God like this, He could only be *revealed*!"

As the weeks passed, extensive tests finally established

the presence neither of cancer nor T.B., but a severe abscess which needed long and painful treatment. "God blessed me with tens and hundredfolds of faith in that time," admitted Vijay later. Shortly after his discharge he attended another lunch-hour at St. Helen's, and was stopped in the porch by a visitor of somewhat extremist beliefs. "Don't you know this place is dead? They never have healings here. There's nothing happening at St. Helen's!" Vijay looked up. "I've just been discharged from hospital after a twenty-week stay," he replied. "My healing was a very slow one, no sudden miracles! But" – he smiled – "I wouldn't have missed that time for anything. They were the best twenty weeks of my life! Do you know," he rushed on, "in that time God gave me the opportunity to be quiet; no trains to catch, no decisions to make in the office, no pressures of life. I was able to read the whole of the Bible for the first time!"

"And what did your questioner say?" I asked.

"He just walked off," said Vijay.

* * *

Barbara the nurse had found Christ. Her experience in Ward 12 had set her on a search which ended in a friend's home. The church youth fellowship, towards which she had been gravitating, was downstairs, noisily concluding one of its evenings. Barbara was talking upstairs with Carol, one of her nursing friends. Simply, and in her own terms, Carol explained what trusting and following Christ in a personal sense meant, and Barbara unhesitatingly committed her life to Him.

* * *

Vijay was standing up in the inaugural meeting of the General Synod. In the presence of the Bishops, Archbishops and clerical and lay leadership of the Church of England he was speaking as an elected representative of his diocese. His speech was warmly received by the Synod members, and was prominently reported in the national press the next day. In the short time since his stay in hospital he had become an enthusiastic member of our church (though maintaining a "lunch-hour membership" at St. Helen's!), and was accepted as a member of Christ's family. He was playing a positive rôle on our church council. Susheila his wife had joined him as a Christian and their children had been baptized. Together they were later to take a key part in a ten-day mission led by our parish in the West Country town of Cullompton. Quite a lot had happened.

* * *

It is Cup Final Day, May 18th, two years after the Ward 12 episode. The Bride and Groom are surrounded by their relatives and friends. The church service is over and a decorous sprinkling of confetti glamourizes the scene. Flash guns are popping right and left. The toastmaster's voice is working overtime. "Raise your glasses, ladies and gentlemen!" he cries, "To the Bride and Groom – John and Barbara!" "John and Barbara" we dutifully echo. Outside Vijay's car, suitably polished for the occasion, is at the ready...

* * *

It wasn't that the rest of us did anything at all in these converging stories. We were simply the interested and enthralled spectators, seeing God at work, and seeing it all largely in retrospect anyway. "If anyone had told me a year earlier," said Vijay, "that I would have over five painful months in hospital and that I would spend them reading the Christian Bible, I would willingly have paid any amount of money and begged my Hindu gods to deliver me from such a fate!"

"If anyone had told me that I would be married to a clergyman one day," laughs Barbara, "I'd have told him to get lost. I always used to regard clergy as a sort of third sex!"

All of which goes to show that God can use anything to bring about His good in people's lives. Even a lost football match.

6

TAUGHT BY PAIN

The telephone rang.

"Is that you, Richard?"

"It is! It sounds like Valerie there."

Christian names are virtually the order of the day in our church fellowship. It just seems more like a proper family that way. Hardly a soul calls me "Vicar". On this Wednesday morning my telephone caller was Valerie Hadert, a girl suffering from multiple sclerosis.

"Guess what, Richard!"

"I can't. You tell me."

"I'm going to help write a book."

"A book? What about?"

"It's about people who have suffered, and what they've learnt through their experience. It's going to be called *Taught by Pain*."[1]

Eventually I was to get my own autographed copy. It was a good title, I reflected, as I came to the end of the book. The problem of pain and suffering is not an issue

[1] Endersbee, M.: *Taught by Pain* (Falcon 1970).

for detached academic debate. It seems that if there are any lessons to be learned about the subject, they really have to be learned pragmatically and from inside personal experience.

My mind goes back to a young humanist's challenge, "How can you believe in a God of love, when you see all the suffering in the world?" It was a special "confrontation" arranged between myself and the local Humanist group. They weren't quite as terrifying as the advance newspaper publicity had suggested. Or as numerous! Why, I'd thought to myself as I entered the hall, our men's singing group alone would soon gobble that little lot up. The Church of England may have lost a third of its communicants in the last decade (most of it dead wood, I would hazard), but a look at a recent annual report of the British Humanist Association discloses a loss of twenty-five per cent in a single year!

However the question of suffering has to be faced. Logically, as I reminded my humanist friend, it is best answered by those who have themselves suffered. Two things amaze me when I meet with such people. The first is the astonishing resilience of the human body and personality. It almost seems as though man thrives on the challenge of adversity. The second is the vast diversity of people who claim to have gained in one way or another through their suffering.

Not that suffering was a part of God's original creation. The creation itself is fallen by reason of the sin and rebellion of man, and the pain and suffering around us are a reminder that "the whole creation has been groaning in travail together" (Romans 8: 22). If sin and suffering are connected, however, it does not necessarily follow that an individual's suffering is a direct consequence of his own sin. This must be remembered when sick people exclaim, "Do you think God is punishing me for my sin?"

The Christian recognizes that affliction and pain are part of our world. But more than that. Tribulation is an integral part of Christian discipleship. In Acts 14: 22 we read of how Paul and Barnabas were "strengthening the souls of the disciples, exhorting them to continue in the faith, and saying that *through many tribulations we must enter the Kingdom of God*". The word "must" is important, surely. We are following in the steps of One Who Himself faced inevitable tribulation and suffering, culminating in a violent death. Challenge is integral to the Christian life.

I have a friend who built himself a little yacht. It looked very fast. And very unstable! "Won't it turn over?" I asked anxiously, "just one puff of wind and you'll be in the drink." He nodded enthusiastically. "I turned her over the first time I took her out," he admitted, "just to see if she'd do it! I built her like that on purpose, you see." Speed, thrills and challenge had been an essential part of the boat's design. Surely here lies the cutting edge of authentic New Testament Christianity. Built into it is the challenge of trials and cost – of whatever kind. For some it may mean misunderstanding and persecution. For others there may be the refining purposes of God at work in the physical sufferings that come their way. So many of us see sufferings and troubles as a dead end. But the Bible treats them repeatedly as a way out, as a gateway to spiritual progress, as part and parcel of the road of discipleship by which "we must enter the kingdom of God". In the Book of Revelation, St John introduces himself to his readers as "I John, your brother, who share with you in Jesus the tribulation and the kingdom and the patient endurance (Revelation 1: 9). In the very sharing of tribulation through patient endurance (as centred and exemplified "in Jesus"), Christians are sharing in something else – the Kingdom! Evidently the tribulation and the Kingdom are wrapped up in the same package. This is how Valerie Hadert seems to see it. In *Taught by Pain*, she wrote, "Yet though, in a sense, my illness has cut me off from normal life, it also led me to the Lord . . . I've certainly been far happier the last ten years with multiple sclerosis than I ever was, healthy and strong, before I knew Him." Which is quite a statement!

Take the case of a much-loved member of the church, Tom by name. For months he had been plagued with circulation problems in his foot. He had already been in hospital for a painful period of treatment and an operation. Back at home there seemed to be little improvement. His foot was in such pain that sleep was virtually impossible at night. Hour after hour he would pace up and down the floor of the front room trying to distract his mind from the searing agony. Tom's foot! Worked on by specialists, prayed over ceaselessly, it occupied much of the thoughts of many of his church friends. I finally stopped telling Tom and Rose his wife that we were praying for them. They knew it well enough.

Eventually Tom went back into hospital and had a couple of toes amputated. More pain followed. A wheelchair. Then sticks. And finally we watched him walking, albeit gingerly, into the mid-week prayer fellowship at the church. It was quite a triumph. At one stage Tom talked to me as I sat on his bed when visiting his home. "I never felt my recovery was meant to be a quick one," he said. "One or two people have told me I ought to have a special healing service, but I don't think that's God's way for me. I feel that this way there's some special lesson for me to learn. Even now" – he looked up – "I'm not fully sure what the lesson is. But I think I'm learning to grow as a Christian." Certainly to all who knew Tom at all closely, it was evident that he was more mature and more solid in his faith, and that Christ had revealed something of Himself and His love in the testing experience of pain and loss.

But human suffering may also be a means by which God's power and grace are demonstrated to others, and nowhere do we find a better example than in the apostle Paul and his "thorn in the flesh". Whatever his weakness was, we learn from 2 Corinthians 12: 8–10 that it was not taken away from him although "three times I besought the Lord about this, that it should leave me; But" – he continues – "he said to me, 'My grace is sufficient for you, for my power is made perfect in weakness'. I will all the more gladly boast of my weaknesses, that the power of Christ may rest upon me."

Here is an example of unrelieved suffering successfully borne through a power that could only be explained on all sides as stemming from God Himself.

My mind here immediately goes to Derek, a young man in his twenties, another sufferer from multiple sclerosis. "I must have cost the National Health Service quite a small fortune; the tax authorities must be going barmy over me!" he once grinned to me from his hospital wheelchair. Paralysed from the waist down, there was a stage when he was near giving up. "Suicide was a very close thing to me at one time," he admits. His exploring of the Christian faith began with the loan of a book, *The Tartan Pimpernel*,[1] by one of the nurses from our church. "That book answered a situation that I was experiencing myself," reflected Derek, who was determined not to accept the Christian message unless he was convinced within himself that it was true. "At first I thought I was being sold an insurance policy!" he confessed. Little by little the jig-saw began to take shape, and eventually Derek was contributing as a convinced Christian to our "Words of Life" programme on the hospital radio.

"What about having a healing service?" The suggestion came up quite naturally from Derek one day. We discussed the matter fully. The most impressive thing was his balanced outlook. "There was a time," said Derek thoughtfully, "when I would have said 'Well, if they can heal my body they can let my soul rot' – though even then" – he hastened to add with a smile – "I knew I was talking out of the back of my head! But to my mind there's no doubt at all about God being able to heal my body. Whether it's His will or not I just wouldn't presume to be able to judge. And" – he went on confidently – "I'm prepared to take it either way. In a sense it seems comparatively unimportant now! At least the healing of my soul has taken place. And after all there's so much you can do from a wheelchair." In this relaxed

[1] Coskie, D.: *The Tartan Pimpernel* (Fontana 1960).

frame of mind Derek, with several of our Church Council and one or two praying friends, joined me in the hospital chapel for a service of anointing and healing.

Prayer for Derek still continues, and while there is, to be honest, no solid evidence of lasting healing to this day, his faith shines brightly with its testimony to the power of God to give dynamic and purpose to a life weakened by paralysis and inactivity. Two young men were admitted to Derek's ward one day. They were puzzled by his buoyancy. "Here are we, fed up to the back teeth after a week," one of them eventually acknowledged, "and there's him, a permanent invalid, smiling away every time we look at him!" Derek refuses to take credit for this. "If you ask me for the cause of my cheerfulness, I can only tell you it's Christ," he states firmly.

But there seems to be yet another facet of suffering and its purposes under God's hand. Some suffering is for the discipline of the soul, for the training of character and for the assimilation of important lessons for life. This again is basic to the Christian way. We learn of Christ Himself that "he learned obedience through what he suffered" (Hebrews 5:8). Here once more is the Biblical idea of tribulation seen as a positive way into blessing rather than as a dead end in itself. So much so that Paul can write, "We rejoice in our sufferings, knowing that suffering produces endurance, and endurance produces character . . ." It's a dangerous thing then to pray for patience. A prayer for patience may be equivalent to asking God for an extra load of troubles!

Come with me in your imagination at this point to meet Win Urry, one of the most patient people I've ever met, and the perfect cure for all grumblers. It's a wet Sunday afternoon in June 1971, as I step through the doorway of Marguerite Ward. With me are two young people, Teresa and Gary, both aged fourteen. Presently Roger, one of my colleagues, and his wife Hilda turn up with another of the church's young people, Melody, aged eleven. Melody is to join the other two as together they record an interview in the ward for Radio London, the BBC local radio station. Somehow or other we had become involved in the production of "The Orange and Lemon Club", a children's weekly half-hour Christian programme of music, drama and interviews. The hospital staff have kindly delayed serving the teas in the ward for a few minutes so that we can have a bit of quiet for the recording. Already the mikes are in place and the Uher battery recorder is at the ready.

"Okay for us to begin now, Win?"

"Yes, ready when you are."

"Right; mind that cable. Now who's going to get the ball rolling? Terry? Stand by then! Off you go!"

"*How long have you been blind now, Win?*"

"Oh, I should think about – fifty years!"

Gradually, through question and answer, Win's story emerges. TB ulcers at the age of twelve were to rob her of her sight. She learnt Braille when she was in her twenties. But then arthritis was to set in, and attacked all her joints. Now in her sixties, she has been bedridden for over twelve years. "I don't bend anywhere. I just can't sit. I'm all the time having to be lifted up because I slide down!" Right back in her teens Win knew that hers was to be a life-long lesson of patience. And faith. The Bible spoke its message to her in Braille over the years. John's Gospel seems to have been to the fore along with several of St Paul's Epistles. The Communion services in the hospital had proved a source of strength as well. No, she never felt lonely. Yes, she was quite contented. The tape spools wound on silently and impersonally. Then to Melody's question "Are you afraid of the future?" Win replied emphatically. "Oh, I look forward to the future more than anything, because I do believe in a life hereafter, and I think that is going to be the best part. I feel then that I shall be free, whereas with this kind of body I feel more like a prisoner!"

"Thank you very much, Win, for letting us talk to you."

"You're welcome dear; I'll see you again one day, I expect." We left her in the ward there, completing another row of knitting, the lady with a reputation for never grumbling.

These are some of the people I'd like our critics to meet; Valerie, Tom, Derek and Win. There are plenty more who, in and through their personal suffering, have encountered the living God, and by their testimony have glorified Him.

7

"THE VICAR'S HERE TO SEE YOU"

"I admire the work that you clergy are doing," said the pleasant-faced Jew in striped pyjamas, "but it's a losing battle your're fighting, isn't it?" That was my cue of course, and I duly took it. But naggingly the thought persisted – Why does the image of the Church remain so persistently bad?

* * *

"Well, it sounds like the old old story of the Church being out of date, but it is!" asserted one critic in his late teens; "you go to this freezing cold place, and it really is freezing cold!"

"And all those people," chimed in his companion, "singing a load of old – well, it's a dirge isn't it? And that old organ – it always seems to stay on the same note, dunnit?"

* * *

Of course there's always the media; that puts us forty-love down for a start! Vicars in TV plays and comedies are predictably behind the times, bumbling and benign. And, let's face it, there are plenty of folk who would like the image to stay like that, so that they can airily banish the Church to a dust-laden pigeonhole marked "Irrelevant", their consciences happily untroubled by the real and eternal issues.

Not that the Church can be let off the hook, mind you. It's worth taking an unhurried critical look around you, next time you go to church. It wouldn't surprise me, or Mr Average Englishman, if the extension was tatty and unkempt, decorated only by a huge red thermometer proclaiming its begging message of woe to the neighbourhood – "£30,000 needed for Tower Restoration".

The porch! It could well be that the first piece of publicity meeting the visitor's eye would be "A Table of Kindred and Affinity", featuring every possible permutation of wierd and horrible marriage entanglements. And inside, there's the furniture, the books, the lighting, the music – and we haven't even got to the Vicar yet, or the choir, or . . .

Naturally there are some very pleasing changes taking place in church affairs today. There *is* plenty of life emerging – young life that believes that Jesus is alive today. There *are* churches that are warm and inviting, radiating fellowship and the love of Christ. But the message hasn't really hit the public yet. And when the Sister whisks down the ward telling a lucky individual – "The Vicar's here to see you," the patient can still only visualize Robertson Hare doing his Archdeacon bit in "All Gas and Gaiters". He really does. And gets a bit of a shock when someone quite ordinary gets shown to his bedside!

One objective then, in hospital visiting, is to do something to alter the musty image of the Church. Not that that is the primary concern. First and foremost the visitor goes as Christ's representative, to minister for Him so that no patient can say "No man cared for my soul". But there is also the long term objective of breaking down barriers, prejudices – and false images, and in today's climate of opinion this may, in fact, constitute the greater part of a chaplain's ministry.

Indeed I tend to be a little chary of "sudden conversions" in hospital. Not that they don't wonderfully happen from time to time. But there is always the danger of a purely emotional change of heart due partly to the peculiarly insulated and introspective outlook that life in a hospital bed tends to generate. Tears come all too easily. Resolves can be swiftly made – and as swiftly forgotten, once health returns.

As a pale thin young curate some years ago, I used to emerge from a couple of hours bed-to-bed visitation sweating all over with the sheer effort of attempting a direct spiritual confrontation with every patient. Nowadays I'm more relaxed. Experience has taught me that although hospital is a great leveller of men, an afternoon's ward visit will bring me into contact with the greatest variety of I.Q.s, reactions and opinions as I'm ever likely to find under one roof. Flexibility is a must in such conditions.

There are days when you feel you're on an emotional switchback. Deep in talk, Bible open at one bed; roaring with laughter and eating the man's grapes at the next! Murmuring a prayer with an anxious soul one moment; bellowing the Gospel to a deaf patient two minutes later. Actually the deaf ones are a blessing in disguise, if broadcasting the Faith to the entire company is desired. You've got to be quite shameless though!

"Have you ever thought of Jesus Christ as a close friend?"

"Pardon?"

"*Have you thought of Jesus as a friend?*"

"Eh?"

"IS JESUS YOUR FRIEND?"

"Wait a minute, I've got a hearing aid somewhere. Can you open my locker?"

And off you go again.

I say this; unless a man is in earnest when it comes to work of this kind, he'd better not begin at all. One of the difficulties, indeed, is in getting stuck into an afternoon's visiting in the first place. When the pressure is on, a dozen different alternative activities will present themselves, and the visiting is always the first thing to go.

Once stuck into it, you've got to admit there's nothing like it for blowing the cobwebs away. This is the real thing. Apart from the sense of privilege at representing Christ's cause, visiting is the perfect therapy for anyone isolated by his pre-occupations or depressed by his own problems.

There was Margaret in Ward 1. All I could see of her, to begin with, was a thin spiral of cigarette smoke rising from behind the *Daily Mirror*. Gradually she put her paper down and began to unwind. "I've been watching your lot," she confided. "In that service you had here on Sunday, I was looking at the faces of those ladies who came along with you; I knew they must be true Christian people. And I've got nothing. How can I be like them?"

Admittedly it isn't always like that. My visits tend to one of two extremes; either I'm having a good day, or an apparently un-productive one. But even on an "off" day there is still the element of challenge present. How best to "wake up" the fellow pretending to be asleep! How to penetrate the armour of the ex-serviceman who only enjoys a good argument? Or even, whether to disturb or leave in peace the two old boys playing dominoes?

If I can, I'll visit the whole ward. The lot. And just see what can be done. I'll take a Bible along in my hip pocket. "Would you like me to read to you from the Bible?" asked Hugh, a clergyman friend of mine, as he stood at the side of a hospital bed. "All right, Padre," came the reply. "You read to me from the Bible." It was the beginning of a spiritual adventure for that middle-aged patient, who was ultimately to become an active church member. Later on he confided, "No parson had ever offered to read the Bible to me before. It started something in me."

There's prayer too. I don't simply mean the mumbling of a collect into a man's ear. Rather, a prayer which, in down to earth language helps to express the hesitations and perplexities of a groping soul – and sometimes unlocks its secrets. Frequently a person's real problem – the block-buster problem – is only finally revealed after the closing prayer of the interview.

Then there's literature. Some hospital chaplains have produced their own newspaper for internal consumption. We finally came up with *Scope*, a special "hospital" edition of a little two-colour, four page mini-paper, produced twice a year for every home in our parish. Designed along the lines of the popular press, it carried details about the hospital's radio programme, its League of Friends, and stories of one and another who, in various ways, had met with God during their hospital stay. And because *Scope* was primarily produced for a tightly-knit community, I can only say that whenever it's been handed around, virtually every patient has read it – on the spot. If it does nothing else, a hospital paper can help the image of Christ's Church, and serve as a confidence-booster for lay and clerical visitors alike, providing them with something to give away, and perhaps providing a talking point too.

Talking points are, in fact, among the many demands made upon the bed-to-bed visitor. Take a maternity ward, for instance. If one's opening gambits are even remotely stereotyped, the occupant of the last bed will automatically have her replies ready and rehearsed! "Boy" – "Yesterday" – "Seven pounds, five ounces" – "Blue" – "Fine, thank you!"

Perhaps this is the danger, that our work can degenerate into a routine of fulfilling our quota of visits, trotting out an acceptable patter and waving the flag perfunctorily before hurrying home to a light supper and "Z Cars". Our Lord must have felt something of this temptation at times. So many people! And yet He always kept fresh His vision and His concern for the individual.

"I had my miracle yesterday!" the lady in Ward 4 told me. "I was in such pain I didn't know where to put myself. 'Oh,' I thought to myself, 'if only the curate Roger would come and see me!' He'd been such a comfort, taking the service when my husband died. 'Please God,' I prayed, 'please send Roger.' I rolled over in bed in my pain and frustration and faced the wall, weeping silently. 'Please God, please send Roger.' I heard a noise behind me. I turned round in bed, looked up, *and there was Roger*. 'Thank you!' I said, 'You don't know it, but you're my answer to prayer!' "

It is this sense, that someone cares, which can make the whole difference for folk who are suffering. Four or five hundred beds will change their occupants on average once every two or three weeks at the very least. That represents several thousand patients a year, coming and going, and each with private hopes, joys, frustrations and sorrows. For one of these to feel that Christ has come alongside, through one of His ambassadors of hope and cheer, is the miracle that supernatural Christianity still makes possible.

8

HEALING: LET'S EXPLODE SOME FALLACIES

"Mummy, what's Daddy doing?"

"Your daddy," said Liz severely, "is busy polishing his toes."

It was true, I regret. I was off to speak at a meeting, and hadn't time to give my shoes more than the most spartan treatment before rushing for the train!

A clergyman's life can be very full, simply by virtue of its diversity. The poor man may find himself as a speaker, writer, social worker, marriage guidance counsellor, publisher, artist, electrical engineer, manager and chief stoker. He's like a juggler, keeping a dozen balls in the air at once, a Jack of all Trades and maybe master of only a few.

I don't pretend to be a specialist on healing. Nevertheless my job guarantees a fair cross section of statements and opinions on this subject reaching me – and not least by the "weirdy magazines" sent to me regularly through the post by mysterious anonymous donors.

Some at least are definitely weirdy, and others fall into an indefinite category where the dividing line between truth and error is hard to discern.

I remember the sense of frustration and disillusionment that built up in one patient I visited in hospital. A faithful member of her church, she had been given a book which was a mixture of half truths and plain error. It was to lead her down a blind alley that lost her the peace of mind she had known, and kept her in a wilderness of doubt and anxiety for a considerable time. It is in a small attempt to save some reader a similar experience that I venture to examine some of the popular fallacies tossed around today.

"*I suppose God is punishing me.*" Umm. People have been saying this from their hospital beds for generations. In fact this sentiment is fairly creaking with age because you find Job's "Comforters" glibly coming out with it way back in the Old Testament; "Behold, God will not reject a blameless man" (Job 8: 20), the implication being that Job *was* blameworthy, and so deserved the deluge of troubles that came his way. And yet in fact God's own description of Job was that "there is none like him on the earth, a *blameless* and an upright man". Certainly there are cases in the Bible of sickness being a punishment – take for instance Miriam's leprosy in Numbers chapter 12. Such cases are, however, very exceptional.

Of course there is a connection between disease and sin in general. Death, and all that contributes to it and goes along with it, came about through the fall of man (Romans 5: 12). Creation itself is fallen (Romans 8: 21); hence the presence of disease, decay and death in our world. And – let's face it – in certain cases a person's particular sin is directly connected with his disease. My mind goes back to the middle aged alcoholic I visited in hospital. His love of the bottle had led directly to disease and subsequently blindness. Or there was the girl of seventeen I was asked to minister to, whose promiscuous way of life as a prostitute had infected her with venereal disease.

But then you take a look at Epaphroditus, one of Paul's honoured fellow-workers who was, apparently, 'ill, near to death". The reason for his illness is given as the work he had been doing for Christ (Philippians 2: 30). Or there was Timothy with his sick stomach and "frequent ailments", who nevertheless is described by Paul as "my true child in the faith". No blame seems to have been attached to him. Certainly the epidemics of history have knocked off saint and sinner alike, and frequently the finest physical specimens you find are by no means Godly in their living. So Job's comforters take heed!

"*I feel I'm letting the Lord down.*" She had a sunny personality, and bore a tremendous Christian witness during her illness – but there it was, a lurking suspicion in the back of her mind that every true Christian should expect to enjoy constant good health. True or false? Completely false!

In point of fact there is no person anywhere who enjoys constant good health. The moment a baby is born there begins a battle against disease and death; at quite an early age we're beginning to decay and fold up; aches and pains begin; teeth develop holes; bones begin to get brittle and vision begins to fail. No Christian is immune from illness, and every Christian faces death. The great Paul himself knew what weakness was, as have other great spiritual leaders such as Henry Martyn. What about the great missionary Amy Carmichael? She was bedridden for the last ten years or so of her life, but she could hardly be called lacking in faith! The fact is that we are still in this life within the gravity pull of the Fall and have yet to experience what the Bible calls "the redemption of our bodies" (Romans 8: 22–23). To believe that "first class discipleship" goes hand in hand with spanking good health is a delusion. You find a somewhat similar delusion at the heart of the Christian Science movement which holds that sin, sickness and death are merely states of mind, and that you have only to believe that you are perfectly well, and simply live and act as though you are. To my mind, to pursue such a line of wishful thinking is bound to reap a later harvest of strain and frustration. I am reminded of that slightly naughty limmerick:

There was a faith healer of Deal
Who said that though pain is not real,
When I sit on a pin and it punctures my skin,
I dislike what I fancy I feel!

Christian Science aside, if a person really thinks that his beliefs demand that he be in top physical condition, he is going to be in for some pretty shattering disillusionments when – as is inevitable – sickness and decay set in. Evidently our Lord's disciples needed correction in their bland assumption that someone's sin lay at the heart of the case of the man born blind. "Who sinned, this man or his parents, that he was born blind?" (John 9: 2). Jesus' reply is illuminating. "It was not that this man sinned or his parents, but that the works of God might be made manifest in him." There then followed the healing of the man, and his subsequent testimony of faith (v. 38).

But some Christian folk sincerely believe that sickness is invariably due to Satanic attack. That such a thing is possible is demonstrated by the story of Job, and also by Paul's description of his own affliction as "a messenger of Satan" (2 Corinthians 12: 7), though we must note that in both cases God permitted such activity and ultimately furthered His own purposes through it. It seems to me, however, an unbalanced reaction to say immediately in the face of illness, "Satan has been having a go at me".

In one of the most honest testimonies I have ever read, the renowned Convention speaker Alan Redpath describes his initial reaction to a stroke he sustained some years ago as being along these lines. But then he writes, "It was then, the first time for months, that it seemed the Lord drew very near to me, though I am sure He was very near all the time, even if I was unconscious of the fact. I had no vision of Him, or any dramatic touch of healing; but I do know that a deep conviction came to my heart, in which He said, 'You have this all wrong. The devil has nothing whatever to do with it. It is Me, your Saviour, who has brought this experience into your life.' " As Alan Redpath acknowledged later, the whole shattering episode was not only to result in the healing of his body, but in the reshaping of his priorities and indeed of his entire ministry.

Illness, far from constituting a "let-down" of the Lord, may in fact be God's chosen way of a fresh encounter with Himself.

But let me move on to another type of fallacy altogether. I see it basically as the product of an unbelieving mind: *Prayer has no effect on outward circumstances – it only affects the mind of the one praying*. True or false? The answer has to be *false*. One of the great examples of prevailing prayer given us is that of Elijah, "a man of like nature with ourselves and he prayed fervently that it might not rain . . . " (James 5: 17). The first thing of interest is that this Old Testament happening is used by James to encourage his New Testament readers to pray for one another, "that you may be healed" (James 5: 16). So evidently outward circumstances are affected through prayer. Secondly, Elijah is not portrayed here as a super saint whose prayers would have more effect than lesser mortals. He is described as "a man of like nature with ourselves". His was the kind of prayer, therefore, that ordinary everyday disciples may pray, with their concern for everyday happenings and circumstances. Thirdly, way back in that Old Testament narrative, the indications seem to be that God was telling Elijah anyway what He was planning to do about the weather (1 Kings 18: 1), and so was virtually praying the prayer through Elijah.

This is important. Real prayer is not an attempt to persuade a reluctant God to bend His action to accomplish our will; rather is it the means He has appointed by which His will can be discovered and brought about in people's lives and circumstances. Furthermore, there seems to be, from what Jesus said, a particular power available through prayer when there is agreement by two or more persons about a common concern (Matthew 18: 19–20). How does this work out practically?

I remember when Ray, our churchwarden, heard on the phone that his five-year-old little girl had been taken ill with meningitis. It happened during our parish week-end houseparty at High Leigh Conference Centre in Hoddesdon one September. What more natural than that the whole church family, well familiarized with Liz' cheeky face, should give itself to prayer? As Ray's wife, Joyce, put it later: "It was tremendous really that over a hundred people who knew Liz should be together at that time. That's part of the thing of being in a church family where people know and care. The doctor had said to me that she was a very sick little girl, and yet the next morning she was a different child."

Rightly, we gave thanks to God for this swift recovery, and yet that incident can't begin to give the full picture. What of the occasions when believing prayer has been offered by many Christians, and healing is not granted? The well-meaning folk who hold that it all hinges on faith forget, perhaps, the solemn reminders all around us of the Fall, and of our appointment with death in this world.

Of course there is Christ! When Jesus came to Lazarus' tomb, He said, "I am the resurrection and the life." There is the *ultimate* triumph, in which all Christians have a share – but this still remains to be made complete. Lazarus was wonderfully raised from the dead in that epic moment of Jesus' ministry – as an illustration and *foretaste* of the ultimate triumph at the end of the age. That doesn't mean that Lazarus would never be ill again, or wouldn't have to face death later on.

What has happened through Calvary is that the *sting* of death has gone; its hopelessness and despair, its utter finality have been destroyed. But it still surrounds us and will continue to do so until Christ's return in glory. And – let's face it – *it is still an enemy!* They can only be ostrich-like Christians who pretend otherwise and try at every set-back and sorrow to anticipate heaven before it comes. Encouragements will come to us, but a pain-free existence has yet to be. "Our Father refreshes us on the journey with some pleasant inns," writes C. S. Lewis, "but will not encourage us to mistake them for home."

May we pray for healing? Certainly, according to the Bible, and any restored sufferer may give thanks that the prayer of faith affects more than simply the mind of the one praying. The sixty-four thousand dollar question is, however, can I *claim* healing as my right, in virtue of Calvary's triumph? Let's keep that one for the next chapter.

9

THE REAL MIRACLE?

The healing meeting was drawing to a close. Peter sat in the chair surrounded by some six leaders. In his thirties, he was on his first trip to America, and here in New York State he had met up with a branch of the "Jesus People" which has jumped into prominence.

"How long has your left leg been shorter than the right?" they'd asked.

"Since childhood."

"We'd like to pray that God will heal your leg right now."

With slight misgivings, Peter had consented, and for some minutes the leaders prayed, gripping his leg tightly, at times shaking it, and meanwhile praying in the "tongues" often associated with the charismatic movement. "After some minutes," reflected Peter, "it was clear they were getting a bit embarrassed, as nothing was happening. So I stopped them, and told them what the real miracle had been."

It had all happened at the age of five. A severe bone

disease. There had been talk of amputation. Ten days on the danger list. A series of operations. And finally through prayer, and the skill of a leading surgeon, the saving not only of the five-year-old's life, but his leg as well.

"That was the real miracle," said Peter, putting his shoe on again, "but I'm grateful to you for your concern." The meeting broke up. One of the younger leaders approached Peter again. "You didn't really believe," he remonstrated a little sharply; "If only you'd had faith . . . "

If only you had faith . . . What a world of frustration and disappointment is compressed into those words. And not only that. "If only you had faith" is, alas, the perfect get-out for those to whom healing amounts virtually to a second Gospel. For them the burden lies largely on the faith of the sufferer as to whether or not healing is granted. Their theology demands this, because of their belief that healing, like forgiveness, is an essential part of the Gospel, available to all who come to the foot of the cross. You can express the fallacy as follows:

Isn't healing provided by Christ through Calvary, the right of every believing Christian? At first sight we would want to sympathize with this belief, especially when backed up by texts such as Isaiah 53:4 – "Surely He has borne our griefs (or sicknesses), and carried our sorrows (or pains)." Is it not also significant, we are told, that only a couple of verses later we read of the coming Messiah in terms of His bearing the iniquity of us all – a clear reference to the cross?

And so? "You must claim by faith your purchased inheritance of healing," say our friends, "it's your blood-bought right, just like forgiveness. It's a basic provision of the Gospel of redemption." It is very understandable that many of us fall to this fallacy. It's such an attractive doctrine for one thing. There also seems to be some scriptural warrant for it. Where does the flaw lie?

The flaw is revealed upon a closer study of the Scriptures. This is always the great saving factor – that the Bible's message holds consistently together, that Scripture interprets Scripture and so corrects the false assumptions we are liable to leap to. When we search the New Testament for the fulfilment of Isaiah 53:4, it confronts us in Matthew 8: 16–17. "That evening they brought to him many who were possessed with demons, and He cast out the spirits with a word, and healed all who were sick. *This was to fulfil what was spoken by the prophet Isaiah, 'He took our infirmities and bore our diseases'.*"

This event, recorded as taking place at Capernaum, is, surely, illustrative of the *Incarnation* rather than the Atonement. Here, in Matthew 8, is portrayed primarily the sympathetic Christ, the God-Man stepping down into our world alongside suffering humanity, rather than the sacrificial Lamb of Calvary. For at the heart of the cross is the idea of *substitution*, as expressed in Isaiah 53: 6, already mentioned – "The Lord has laid on him the iniquity of us all." Similarly, Mark 10: 45, where our Lord speaks of Himself as giving "his life as a ransom for (literally 'instead of') many". Again in 2 Corinthians 5: 21 – "For our sake he made him to be sin who knew no sin."

In other words, if men were to be spared from drinking the cup of guilt for their own sins, that same cup had to be drained by our Lord instead, and indeed this took place at the cross. But when it comes to Matthew 8: 16–17, that substitutionary element, inherent in Calvary, is missing. As the commentator Alfred Plummer observes, "It at least must mean that Christ removed their sufferings from the sufferers. *He can hardly have meant that the diseases were transferred to Christ.* But we may understand him as meaning that Christ's sympathy with the sufferer was so intense that He really felt their weaknesses and pains." Which expresses beautifully the truth of the Incarnation. But this is quite different from the Atonement and Calvary. The Cross is unique as the means by which the penalty of our sins was removed and transferred to Christ.

Calvary did not buy every Christian the right to be healed physically, any more than it bought us the right to escape the approach of physical death. As that practical Bible expositor Guy King once logically remarked, "Not all Christians are to be healed; else, how should we ever die?"

There is, of course, that positive passage in James 5: 14–15, with its provision for a sick person to ask the church leaders to come and pray with him (and note that the sick person is the one to do the asking – not a pressing well-wisher!). Even there the phrase "and the prayer of faith will save the sick man" seems deliberately ambiguous. "Save" may mean healing now, or full salvation later, beyond this life. On the several occasions when we have held such times of prayer with sick people, we have simply placed the matter in the hand of God, refusing to dictate times or terms to Him.

Surely this is biblical.

When we examine the preaching of the New Testament, we look in vain for evidence that the apostles ever preached that all should be healed as well as forgiven. Paul himself was left with this "thorn in the flesh", and he writes in 2 Timothy 4:20, "Trophimus I left ill at Miletus." Why was this believer left unhealed if Paul's Gospel demanded otherwise? Especially if Paul possessed a gift of healing, as evidenced on more than one occasion?

Not that the healings of the New Testament weren't important! Particularly do they appear to have had an authenticating value as the Kingdom of God began its New Testament course. When John the Baptist sends from prison for proof of Christ's identity, the messengers are told, "Go and tell John what you have seen and heard; the blind receive their sight, the lame walk, lepers are cleansed, and the deaf hear, the dead are raised up, the poor have good news preached to them" – a clear reference to Isaiah's prophecies of the coming Deliverer.

Elsewhere our Lord's miracles are greeted by such reactions as "God has visited His people", and "Truly you are the Son of God", and of course John's emphasis in the fourth Gospel upon the miracles being "signs" pointing to Christ's identity is well known. Look on, and in the Acts we discover that the apostles' miracles are similarly seen as an authentication of the authority of the messengers, as in Acts 4:10.

Today when we hear of miraculous healings, the reports generally seem to stem from some pioneer outpost of the Christian Gospel, and I do not believe that this is an accident. We needn't shrug cynically when we hear of them, even though for the most part scientific verification will not be available. Missionaries down the ages have acknowledged God's frequent provision and over-ruling in areas where hospitals and medical science have yet to be established. More importantly, the pattern seems to be that miracles of healing have been commonest in any new phase or extension of God's Kingdom, particularly where the Bible is unknown and where God's servants require authentication before a pagan community. That does not rule out the possibility of them happening in our environment today, and during times of spiritual refreshing, but generally the *missionary* areas seem to be those with the greatest frequency of miraculous healing. Let me move on.

"*Surely all healing is the work of God.*" So said the chaplain of an English healing centre as I conversed with him during a visit. "What about the use of white magic?" I had asked. He looked puzzled.

"White magic?"

"You know," I said, "the use of charms, magical fetishes or rod and pendulum."

"Well, we don't quarrel with that; anything can be used if it leads to the healing of someone."

His reply did not surprise me, as I had already conversed with a man at that centre who was receiving treatment with the use of a pendulum.[1] And indeed in a

[1] Dr Kurt Koch writes: 'Historically the employment of rod and pendulum has its roots in the soothsaying of heathendom. The Mosaic and prophetic religion of Israel consequently carry on a vigorous battle against the adoption of these heathen-mantic practices' – *Christian Counselling and Occultism* (Kregel Publications 1965, page 81).

culture shaped by centuries of Christian tradition it is not surprising to find the widespread bland assumption that all healing is the work of God.

We forget that in pagan lands healing has been the practice of witch-doctors over many generations, and certainly in the country areas of East Africa where I was brought up as a boy, many villages had their own *mundu-mugo* to whom folk would come seeking a cure for their ailments. It seems that at least some occult and heathen attempts at healing have not been without results either, despite the presence of charlatans and phonies in this field.

Results or no, Scripture is clear in its condemnation of all mediumistic activity, contact with the world of the dead, and use of magical devices.[1] My own experience of counselling those even remotely involved in occult practices is that depression and a growing distaste for the things of God appear to be unhappy by-products of such activities.

Where does the dividing line come, between the crank and the genuine, when seeking the healing touch of God? Dr Kurt Koch of Germany, a known world authority on Christian counselling in the field of occultism, states that genuine prayer for healing begins to degenerate and teeter on the edge of the mediumistic once an attempt is made to "force a result". At that point the issue is no longer trustingly left in the hands of the heavenly Father Who cares and acts for His children. It has been taken out of His hands, and the one praying –

[1] See, for example, 1 Chronicles 10: 13–14; Isaiah 8: 19–22 and Acts 19: 18–19. Hosea 4: 12 may be a reference to rhabdomancy – the use of divining rods, which frequently goes hand in hand with the use of pendulum.

wittingly or unwittingly – begins (to use Koch's phrase) to "plug in below". Religious phrases may still be used – but that's just it; they are being *used.* The Lord's name may be employed, virtually as a charm or magic formula. No longer is the would-be healer humbly submitting himself to the will and power of God; he is now in the driving seat.

Perhaps this is the most helpful approach in exercising discernment when it comes to the numerous healing movements that are sweeping the world today, many of which at least purport to be Christian and biblical in orientation. The more a healer shouts and presses, the more he offers guarantees and results, the bigger the photographs and banner headlines of dramatic healings, the faster do I switch off. For man now seems to be at the centre, and the "gift", if it is a gift, appears to have become the gospel.

The glorious thing about the New Testament healings was that they seemed to be a spontaneous by-product of something bigger. Here is Paul busy in the expansion of the swiftly-growing Church. The power and excitement mount, and spill over – to the extent that at one stage even handkerchiefs that have been in contact with the great apostle appear to have healing qualities adhering to them, and for a while there is one great mad rush for these wonder-working hankies as they're passed fervently from hand to hand!

Today, sadly, we are faced increasingly with the "Send-us-two-dollars-and-we'll-send-you-a-handkerchief" brigade. Even more sadly, the folk most in need of genuine Christian help are frequently those most vulnerable to an approach which, at its best is misguided zeal, and at its worst is a pretty obnoxious form of commercial exploitation.

One might let pass some minor extravagancies if there was more evidence available of lasting healing, beyond simply a photograph and a story. I have a doctor friend who determined to carry out a study of some of these reported healings. He selected, first of all, a report from one of the most well-known healing movements. The magazine photograph depicted a boy giving away his crutches. This had been hailed as a triumph of healing. My friend wrote to the magazine's headquarters, stating that he was undertaking some study in the field of healing, and might he have the address of the boy's parents? He was given the address, and went to visit the home, only to discover that although the boy's parents had indeed sought for a cure from the healer concerned, there had been no improvement whatsoever resulting from the visit to the healing meetings. Such good as had been done had been achieved during a three month period in hospital.

"I must give the movement another chance," thought the doctor. Accordingly he selected another dramatic story in the following month's magazine. He wrote for the address, only to be given the brush-off by the directors, who requested him curtly to cease interfering with the work of the organization. Perhaps this illustrates something of the difficulty involved in trying to make an accurate assessment of the success or otherwise of the healing movements. Suffice it to say that there are grounds for some disquiet.

For another remarkable thing about the New Testament healings is the very authority with which they were accomplished. There was no denying what had happened. No "Is-he-well-or-isn't-he?" uncertainty. Furthermore there was no preoccupation with miraculous cures for coughs and colds, toothache and in-growing toenails, as seems common in some circles today. Presumably on the apostles' travels, Luke, "the beloved physician", was able to do his bit, and there is no evidence in the New Testament that the life of faith is in any way incompatible with the use of medicine. Indeed the development of medicine in history is surely a part of man's fulfilment of the divine command to subdue the earth and to govern its resources.

Where there were miracles in the New Testament, it was invariably a major matter that was put right, and put right with such authority that no doubt was left in anybody's mind. The healing miracles of Jesus were, with one exception, instantaneous, and there is no record of any relapses taking place.

John, a Christian, was attending a healing meeting in the north of England. Earlier in the week a certain lady had been pronounced cured of her ailment – had discarded the walking support upon which she had hitherto depended, and had gone home. Today, thanksgiving to God was being expressed for this "miraculous healing". However, when the time for healing came in that same meeting, with the laying on of hands, *there she was again with the other enquirers*, complaining that she was not as fit as she ought to have been.

The leader's diagnosis was, "She just needs assurance". There was in fact great uncertainty as to whether anything had taken place. Following a further laying on of hands, the same lady was called out to the front to demonstrate that she had now really been healed. "She was literally staggering," recalled John, the eyewitness, "and liable to collapse. I was very near her, and it was all I could do to refrain from rushing out to the front to give her some assistance." His comment upon this healing meeting – "I felt quite ill afterwards."

Certainly such a tragic episode could never have been the healing associated with Jesus and the apostles. It lacked – authority. I share these descriptions not for the sake of negative criticism, but to warn the gullible against the pain and disillusionment that could result from believing that all healing is the work of God. And who of us is not gullible? I have room for a last fallacy in this chapter:

Unless the Church performs more astounding miracles than our Lord did on earth, it is failing its Lord. This assertion, in various forms, has been made throughout Christian history, largely because of one verse in the New Testament. It is John 14: 12 – "Truly, truly, I say to you, he who believes in me will also do the works that I do; and greater works than these will he do, because I go to the Father."

A good deal of misunderstanding has surrounded these words, as far as I can judge. A little thought will remind us that in fact throughout history no apostles or disciples ever did accomplish more astounding deeds in the physical realm than did the Son of God. After all, what genuinely authenticated accounts have we of apostles or disciples stilling a storm with a word, feeding several thousand people from virtually nothing, healing at a distance, or raising from the dead after four days in a grave? What hits us immediately, as we read of Jesus' miracles in the Gospels, is the sheer magnitude of His miraculous deeds – and also their frequency. Move on a few pages into the Acts of the Apostles, and already there seems a definite decrease in such deeds, both in quality and quantity.

Perhaps what we have missed in the John 14:12 passage, has been the significance of the last few words. "Greater works than these he will do," Jesus had said, "*because I go to the Father.*" Here surely lies the clue to the meaning of His prophecy. With the withdrawal of Christ's immediate presence from earth, would begin the era of the Spirit, inaugurated on the day of Pentecost. By "greater works", our Lord surely was not referring to deeds of a superior physical quality so much as to *deeds of a superior dimension altogether*. The new age was to be the age of the Spirit, as men and women in Palestine, then Asia Minor, Europe and across the world were to be introduced to the spiritual life available in the risen and glorified Christ. The miracle of new birth by the Spirit was to be achieved in human lives on a global scale, life-changing in its effects, all-energizing in its power. And all through ordinary, humble believers. Greater works? Indeed yes.

The difficult thing always with miraculous healing is to see it in its right perspective. Most of us have newspaper headline type of minds; we're dazzled by the spectacular, the fantastic. The following story illustrates the kind of emphasis that should govern our thinking. It was told in my hearing by Festo Kivengere of Uganda, the world-travelled evangelist and visitor to revival areas all over the world:

"This happened in 1962. A cripple who never walked came to a fellowship meeting – not a healing meeting. He was a member of a little church in the village. Hearing people singing in the afternoon he crawled in as usual. Under the conviction of the Spirit in this revival area of East Africa, he sat with those twenty-five men and women, as they prayed, sang praise and read the Bible. With tears streaming down his cheeks, he turned and he said, 'I want to accept the Lord Jesus.' One of the leaders said, 'Get up and accept Him.' And the cripple literally got up, legs and all, to the amazement of the Christian who had told him to! And he gave a lovely testimony of how God had liberated him and forgiven him his sins, and towards the end he looked down at his legs and said, 'And as if that was not enough, He has straightened my legs!' Later my wife and I gave this fellow a lift in our car, and we saw him walking home. It was a downright New Testament miracle, but our joy was not because the legs were straightened – he was bound to die anyway later on. We were rejoicing over another miracle, the miracle of the new life, which was never to die again. That is the greatest miracle."

10

UNSTRUCTURED OPPORTUNITIES

Slowly, reluctantly, I crawled back to consciousness as the telephone bell jangled stridently by my ear. Apprehensively I fumbled for the receiver in the darkness. Telephone calls at one a.m. rarely bring good news.

"Yes?"

"Mr Bewes?" A girl's voice. The accent was foreign. "This is the Maternity special care unit. Would you come and take a baptism for us here please?"

A baptism. At midnight!

"Er, how urgent is it?" I gulped.

"Oh, it's quite urgent." The girl's voice sounded bright and perky. "There is some anxiety about one of the babies here and . . . "

"Right, I'll be along in a minute." Instant obedience, Bewes, I thought, as I put the receiver down. Remember you're on night call.

"Who is it?" asked Liz sleepily.

"Hospital," I explained shortly. "They want me to go

and do some baptisms!" I reached for my clerical collar, a clammy piece of clothing at anytime, but at one a.m ... "I wonder if they think that because I'm on night call I'm primly sitting up all night in my cassock, waiting to be called?" In spite of myself I began to giggle.

But once in the special care unit a few minutes later, any sense of irritation was swept away as I peered at the shrimp-like thing in the incubator. Less than two pounds in weight. A little girl. Someone brought a bowl of water. I completed the simple baptism and then prayed as the staff nurse stood by. "Dear Lord, let Sharon grow up to be strong and well. Help her parents to bring her up as a Christian. And in later life let her be reminded of her baptism here in this special care unit."

Back in the car I thought once again of my broken night. "Lord, was I really ordained to be doing baptisms at midnight?" Like a flash I received my answer. "What about Paul? He baptized a whole family at midnight. *And* when he was in a cell after being beaten up." Thoughtfully I put the car away, crept upstairs, and tiptoed into the children's bedrooms for a moment. All three were breathing quietly in the cool night air. That special care unit had been so unbelievably baking hot... In our own room Liz was asleep. Silently I slid myself into bed again and turned over. Thank you God – for everything.

There is so much in this kind of work that is outside the scope of any tidy bureaucratic line of procedure. The work is what you make it. Frequently you have to improvise and use your own initiative. The greatest problem as always is time. You simply cannot sort out certain human tangles and emergencies without hours of talk, scratching around for a solution, and patient negotiation.

I'll always remember Mebra. Mebra was an African girl who had just flown in to begin her training at our hospital, leaving her husband back at home. No sooner had she arrived in England, however, than she discovered that she was expecting a baby. It was Hermione Baker of the Overseas Commendation Centre in London who rang me up to tell me about it.

Hermione Baker! The perfect example of a Christian worker in the right niche. A person of great presence, tireless energy and wide vision, she seemed to make every overseas visitor within reach her own particular responsibility. An overseas nurse would arrive in England, and, lo and behold, telephones would start buzzing, cars would be despatched to Heathrow to meet the plane, while an armada of vicars, social workers and matrons would be prodded tactfully into activity, hunting for suitable accommodation for the new visitor.

Mebra and her baby; it seemed that there was no ready-made machinery to cover her case. The bulk of her time in England was now going to be spent in awaiting the baby's birth, and then in rearing the new arrival. Accommodation was the main difficulty. I have a file in my study, marked "Accommodation Problems". Most such problems never get solved. Mebra's was solved finally by two members of our congregation; one offering to accommodate her up to the time of the baby's birth, the other to take over from that point on. All went well, and Mebra settled down into the church fellowship. Little Richard was finally born safely, and his baptism took place at the evening service one Sunday, with several church members standing by as god-parents. There seemed to be one additional figure near the font as I approached. It was – inevitably – Hermione Baker.

Next there was the problem of getting Mebra back to Africa! No money was available, it seemed. The only thing to do was to have a whip-round among some of the church family, and this we did. The close of the story came in July, 1972, with a telephone call from Hermione Baker. Yes, Mebra was happily back with her husband. Little Richard was thriving. And – a cheque had been sent to Hermione to repay the air fare provided by Christian friends in England. Er . . . about the cheque – did we want the money back, or would we like it to be made available for a similar case!

Having responsibility both in the hospital and in the nearby parish church has, of course, its advantages. I try to remember this when lecturing, as I occasionally do, to the Preliminary Training School nurses. Every spiritual link outside the hospital is to be encouraged. I remember Jenny's arrival at the Vicarage one day. I'd never really known her up till then. "Can you give me some job to do in my off-duty periods?" she'd asked. "Maybe help some old person in the neighbourhood?"

I thought rapidly. "Yes, there is something you can do. There's a dear old lady who's dying to go and hear Billy Graham at Earl's Court. Do you think you could organize a wheelchair for her, take her on the coach and look after her for the evening? She's Mrs Campbell of 40 Geoffrey Avenue." I then paid a quick visit to Geoffrey Avenue. "Mrs Campbell, I think I've got someone to take you to Earl's Court. A nurse from the hospital. Jenny's her name. You will pray for her during the evening, won't you"? Our gentle subterfuge worked, and by the end of the month Jenny was declaring herself to be a follower of Christ. As I write now, she's serving God in a hospital in Kenya.

Others have come and gone during their period of training; Carol, now a clergyman's wife; Nell, a Dutch girl who began her life as a Christian during her time in England; Jane, Mary, Helen, and a whole list of unpronounceables from the West Indies, Africa and Malaysia.

Within the walls of many hospitals there is plenty to help and stimulate Christian fellowship and discussion among the staff, and, notably for the nurses, there is the Inter-Hospital Nurses' Christian Fellowship, which runs its own magazine and holds conferences and evening get-togethers. The I.H.N.C.F. was run for years in London by Alice Hoare, an indefatigable Christian worker who appeared to spend all day doing personal counselling, and all night typing shoals of letters to nurses throughout the length and breadth of England. Talk of unstructured opportunities! Alice Hoare's work fitted into no recognizable "structure" whatever. It was all done on the grapevine – a glorious "adhocracy".

Perhaps this is the common pattern about all that is best in the work of God. Committees and structures there must be, but the impetus and generating power largely stem from individuals of vision and dedication, working flat out in dusty little offices here and there. These are the resilient ones, the Alice Hoares and

Hermione Bakers, who can set a dozen different wheels in motion without turning a hair. These are the opportunists, who see in the ever-increasing flow of overseas immigrants – nurses, doctors and the rest – a harvest field, a God-given missionary opportunity on our own doorstep.

Let me tell you about Koonsang who, like Mebra, met with us and the Christian Gospel in a way that was untidy, unplanned, unstructured, to say the least. He was Chinese, aged forty, had come from a little village near Hong Kong to seek a living in England and pay off the family's debts. He had been working in a restaurant for some months, and then had been taken ill. Really ill.

When I first saw him I was doing bed-to-bed visiting on his ward, and he looked desperately ill. But when I approached him he waved me away, and I had to move on. The same thing happened when I next passed by. I felt terribly for him. Thousands of miles from home in a strange hospital, with a poor command of English. Probably without Christ. Alone and dying. It was, I think, during my third visit that he let me speak to him. He was terribly weak, and I didn't think he had long to live. I must be as simple and direct as possible, I thought.

"Do you know of Jesus?" I enquired. He shook his head. Koonsang's understanding of English was poor, and I had to go very slowly, with frequent pauses to try and show what I meant, by means of mime and gesticulation. I pulled out a little Gospel of John and wondered where to turn. Why not John 3:16? It would probably be the only Bible verse he would ever hear read. Slowly I read it out, pausing now and again to answer a query from the patient. I strove for simplicity as I explained the greatest sentence in the Bible.

> "For God so loved the world that he gave his only Son, that whoever believes in him should not perish but have eternal life."

Several times we were held up by waves of nausea which engulfed the sick man, and then he would recover a little and give his attention to the message again. Slowly, so slowly, the light penetrated. I could see it happening. I then said, "Koonsang, put your name into this message – 'God so loved *Koonsang* that he gave his only Son, that if *Koonsang* believes in him *Koonsang* should not die, but *Koonsang* should have eternal life' ". More minutes passed. "Do you believe this?" I challenged. "Can you believe this for yourself?"

There was a pause. The Chinese man looked at me, then beckoned for the little Gospel of John. "Show me." I showed him the verse we had been talking about. He then reached for a ballpoint pen on his locker, and carefully put a bracket round verse 16. Then deliberately he put a tick in the margin. Another look. His meaning was unmistakable, but I questioned him again. "What do you mean by this?"

"I believe", he replied. "I believe. Thank you. You came to help me. Thank you for helping me. I believe." It was moving. As our conversation stumbled on I could see that it had really happened. The sick man was gratitude itself. He was so grateful that he put both arms around my neck, refusing to let go. Not that it was me he had to thank. God had done it all – had simply opened his understanding through the one Bible verse he was ever going to read.

We prayed. Presently I talked of baptism. Koonsang nodded. We fixed this for the following day. The little service was simple in the extreme, attended by the ward sister (a Baptist herself), a staff nurse from our church, and Robbie, my next-door neighbour, who had also paid Koonsang a visit. "I believe, I believe, I believe, I believe. You – my brother!" It was the last time we heard him speak.

Koonsang's things were sent on to his widow. With them I enclosed the little John's Gospel, and a letter in which I tried to express something of what we had talked about in that hospital ward. Did the letter ever arrive? And was there anyone to interpret it at the other end? I shall never know. It was at least my duty – and an opportunity.

II

MEDICINE AND MOTIVATION

Five thousand feet up in the Kenya highlands, the winding muddy road looked completely unchanged from twenty years back. I was nearing the C.M.S. mission station of Weithaga, some seventy miles from Nairobi. Invited as overseas speaker to the "Keswick" Conventions of Tanzania and Kenya, I had put aside a week in order to visit the home I'd known as a boy.

There was Weithaga church – unchanged, except that the bell tower had apparently fallen off! There was our old house, the same yellow soapstone colour, with the red corrugated iron roof. How small it looked now, I thought. And there was the same dear old dispensary! It looked as though it was no longer in use. There's probably something better now, I thought.

Try and imagine your own neighbourhood, gentle reader, minus hospital, minus doctor, minus dentist, minus Boots, minus telephone, gas, electricity, post office, trains, bus service and petrol station. Now transplant it to the top of a hill bang opposite Mount Kenya, and there you have Weithaga, with its wattle and banana trees, its tropical birds and simple agricultural life. Oh, and its dispensary.

My main memories of that tiny dispensary as a boy were of iodine, lint and bandages. There were no antibiotics then of course. For anything more than the simplest ailments, a trip would be necessary into Fort Hall, some twenty miles away, or into Nairobi itself. This, along a dirt track, memorable only for the size and profusion of its "irregularities" in the dry season, and the glutinous quality of its fathomless mud during the rains. But then "Dad's good in mud!" we always prided ourselves.

There was the time when one African patient had to accompany our whole family into town one day. I still recall my surprise on seeing the sick man occupying the entire spacious rear of the Ford V8 Boxbody, while all six of us were jammed like sardines into the driver's section – even under the dashboard – along with yet a seventh passenger, Oswald Wigram, one of the heftiest missionaries in Kenya. It was only later that my parents told us that the man in the back had bubonic plague!

That old boxbody took a fair beating, it really did. Babies delivered in it, lives were saved through it – and all by missionaries whose knowledge of medicine amounted to little more than First Aid. Looking back, an awful lot hung on the services of that dispensary . . .

Naturally knowledge and techniques have come a long way since those precarious earlier times. "You'd never recognize this as the place where Paul White had his 'Jungle Doctor' experiences!" said the Australian matron of Mvumi Hospital in Tanzania, during my two-day stay there. The place was well-staffed and the equipment was modern, to be sure. But in one respect there was no difference. People were still meeting with Christ at this missionary hospital.

Yesu Anipenda. I read the embroidered words on a piece of cloth held up for me by a girl of twelve undergoing physiotherapy. She had done the work herself. *Jesus loves me.* For her the words were apt enough. She had been brought in to the hospital from her pagan environment, more dead than alive. With love and care she had been nursed slowly back to health by the Christian nurses over a period of many months, and in that time had learnt for the first time of a Saviour who had died for her sins and wanted to be her living Friend. For all this she had paid nothing, had been asked for nothing.

The same Christian family atmosphere prevailed at Hombolo leprosy settlement, some little way from Mvumi. To get there you travel virtually through a dustbowl, characterized mainly by thorny scrub and those incredible baobab trees of Tanzania, with trunks of sometimes twenty or thirty feet in circumference. The roads are corrugated, the soil erosion fantastic. But once there, the visitor can swiftly relax in the easy atmosphere and Christian fellowship offered by Dr Guy Timmis and George Hart, the farm manager, together with their families and colleagues. It doesn't take long to see beyond the new buildings and up-to-date laboratories, to the people who have given their lives to work of this kind. George Hart had been at it since 1951. . . .

It was at Hombolo that I first met Denis Burkitt, who was also on a visit. I didn't realize it then, but

Denis Burkitt is a household name in the world of medicine. He probably knows as much as anybody in the world on the subject of the epidemiology of cancer in which he specializes while working for the Medical Research Council. And the "Burkitt Tumour", which derives its name as a result of his findings, is known by medical men across the globe. It was fascinating to talk to this genial-hearted Christian, and to learn something of his experiences gained by visiting hospitals all over the world. I must get this man to preach for us back in England one day, I resolved. And I did.

"Most of us are basically selfish", explained Denis Burkitt some months later in England. He had been jetting around the world and had just arrived from India. And now I was questioning him about motives for the benefit of his audience. "Most of us are basically selfish", he emphasized. "Doctors and other people – of whatever race – tend to work where the amenities are best and where promotion and prospects are good. Unless" – he smiled – "they have some ulterior motive. And in Africa I can say in all honesty that I don't know any area where men or women have worked for long periods in difficult lonely circumstances, other than those of various Christian faiths. Such people are motivated by a love of Christ and through that, a care of others."

In a thousand different hospitals, medical centres and makeshift dispensaries the pattern is the same, in capital city and obscure backwater alike. There may be a touch of adventure about doing a year's Voluntary Service Overseas. But this is different. I recall meeting with Dr Helen Roseveare after her traumatic experiences as a prisoner in the hands of the Simba soldiers during the rebellion of some years back. We met in Kenya, and later when on leave we got her to speak to the crowded young people's meeting at the Keswick Convention in the Lake District. It was a moving experience to see her diminutive figure on the platform, faced by some two thousand of the younger generation. "They took away our belongings", she told the meeting, "they took away our money, they took away our clothes, they took away our dignity and they took away our purity. But they couldn't take Jesus from us. In that we felt completely at one with our African Christian friends who had suffered so terribly and were left with nothing. It was a privilege to suffer with them – for His sake." As I write, Helen Roseveare is back in Zaire once again.

The twentieth century has once again stripped the medical missionary scene of all semblance of glamour and sentimentality. The stark facts presented by the media have seen to that, while the statistics alone are enough to daunt the most optimistic spirits. A 1971 survey revealed that for the ten million people inhabiting the Yemen, there were precisely three hundred and fifty hospital beds available. A 1972 report revealed that in Bangladesh, a land no bigger than Scotland, there were herded together some seventy-five million people, with just six hundred and ninety nurses for the lot of them.

This book has been about Christ and the hospital. The two must always be found together. And if the graph of change means anything, the indications from around the world are that the next few years will see the graph line moving right off the chart altogether. Into the path of Christ's people will be swept a flood of life's casualties, the displaced, the homeless, the wounded and the depressed. It will be impossible to shut our eyes to them, for our world is now a global village. We can be sure that within the tangles of human suffering and sickness there will be a fellowship, an international caring fellowship of doctors, nurses, orderlies, ministers and visitors. Linking them invisibly across the continents will be the spirit that motivated Christ's original band as they went out to heal and to reconcile in a world of danger and spiritual turbulence. Members of that fellowship are not long in recognizing each other. For characterizing them always must be, an eye for the Kingdom, and a love for the King.

JESUS AND THE STREET PEOPLE

A firsthand Report from Berkeley

CLAY FORD

Of the many books to emerge from the youth culture of contemporary America telling of Christian activity and evangelism – this must rate at the least exaggerated and the most helpful. Clay Ford went as a young theological student to share his faith with the 'street people' of Berkeley. He kept a frank and self-critical diary of his efforts and the people he met.
The diary is what we have published.

Here is a book to cure your despondency! *The Christian Herald*
Refreshingly honest. *Nigel Goodwin*

JESUS IS ALIVE AND WELL
The Truths Behind the Stickers and Slogans
BOB OWEN

The youthful upsurge of enthusiasm for Jesus in Britain and America is well known and often reported. Bob Owen has seen it happening.
But this book moves on from the enthusiasm and spells out racily the *doctrines* and meaning of Jesus. It is full of simple, clear teaching. An ideal 'textbook' for young people's Bible studies and for giving to those new to Christian belief.
Reads like a thriller

Its prime virtue is that it makes doctrine exciting reading . . . as a teaching manual for young people, there are very few better books around. *Crusade*